*A Chef's Book of*

# FAVORITE
# CULINARY
# QUOTATIONS

AN INSPIRED COLLECTION
FOR THOSE WHO LOVE TO COOK
AND THOSE WHO LOVE TO EAT

*SG Séguret*

Hatherleigh Press is committed to preserving
and protecting the natural resources of the earth.
Environmentally responsible and sustainable practices
are embraced within the company's mission statement.

Visit us at www.hatherleighpress.com and register online
for free offers, discounts, special events, and more.

## A Chef's Book of Favorite Culinary Quotations

Text Copyright © 2021 SG Séguret

Library of Congress Cataloging-in-Publication Data is available.

ISBN: 978-1-57826-854-2

Printed in the United States

10 9 8 7 6 5 4 3 2 1

# Contents

# Eating:
# A Universal Joy

IN TODAY'S UNCERTAIN WORLD, there's one thing we can still count on. We all eat.

In fact, I would make the case that we spend nearly every moment of our lives wrapped up in some aspect of the pursuit of nourishment. Food is one of the indisputable necessities of our existence, along with air, water, and (to add an intangible) love.

We devote our youth to educating ourselves, so that we might find a job which will permit us to buy food to feed ourselves and our family. We devote most of our waking hours (on top of earning a living so we can buy food) to shopping, cooking, serving, eating, and cleaning up afterwards.

Throughout time, chefs, philosophers, lovers, farmers, and passionate citizens of the world have offered up their thoughts on the subject of nourishment and the various forms its pursuit can take.

This collection reflects the wisdom of these visionaries, who come from so many different walks of life, united in their mutual appreciation of the culinary arts. You are hereby invited to plunge into this gustative richness with abandon, while reflecting on these words of M.F.K. Fisher:

"First we eat, then we do everything else."

# Nourishment

*From the moment we draw our first breath (a form of nourishment in itself), we seek to feed ourselves, be it at our mother's breast or whatever we are lucky enough to grasp. Culinary icons such as Brillat-Savarin, Curnonsky and Michael Pollan, among others, reinforce this quest as our basic "raison d'être".*

The fountain of youth is in your kitchen.

—Paraphrased from DR. JOHN LA PUMA

Food is the first way of gaining energy. Food must be appreciated, savored, in order for its energy to be truly absorbed. This makes eating a holy experience.

—JAMES REDFIELD

Every chef should have to work on a farm for a year before setting foot in the kitchen.

—DARINA ALLEN

Buy foods that look most similar to their original form.

—DR. JOHN LA PUMA

Eating well is a critically important life skill.

—MICHAEL POLLAN

There is no better expenditure of time than that devoted to leisurely partaking of the greatest blessing conferred on man—food.

—HARRY J. JOHNSON

Yummy is important. People eat foods, not nutrients.

—DR. GRANDMA

Food is the most powerful medicine we've got.

—DR. JOHN LA PUMA

Gastronomy is the rational study of all related to man as he is eating. Its purpose is to keep humankind alive with the best possible food.

—BRILLAT-SAVARIN

We taste food using all our senses, emotions, past experiences, religion, and culture.

—CORDON BLEU ATLANTA

When shopping for fruits and vegetables, use at least three senses: sight, touch, and smell.

—DR. JOHN LA PUMA

They're not going to eat it, no matter how healthy it is, if it doesn't taste good.

—SAM KAAS

When you grow a vegetable yourself, you're less likely to boil it to death.

—DARINA ALLEN

The quality and quantity of food consumed exerts a powerful influence on work, rest, sleep, and dreams.

—BRILLAT-SAVARIN

Food should feast the eyes as well as the stomach.

—JAPANESE PROVERB

Cuisine is when things taste like themselves.

—CURNONSKY

Texture is an important part of food appreciation.

—DR. JOHN LA PUMA

I want there to be no peasant in my kingdom so poor that he is unable to have a chicken in his pot on Sundays.

—HENRY IV OF FRANCE

A happy cook makes happy food.

—TRES HUNDERTMARK

Your kitchen is the heart of your health.

—DR. JOHN LA PUMA

Let food be thy medicine and medicine be thy food.

—HIPPOCRATES

Using your knife and fork can save your life.

—DR. JOHN LA PUMA

Real food doesn't have ingredients. Real food *is* ingredients.

—JAMIE OLIVER

The world is nothing without life, and all that lives takes nourishment.

—BRILLAT-SAVARIN

# Cooking

*The act of cooking is one of the most elemental activities we can engage in, and one of the most satisfying, particularly if entered into with joy and celebration. Here, familiar chefs such as Julia Child, Jacques Pépin, Thomas Keller and James Beard, among others, reflect on their passion in the kitchen.*

Cooking is so much more than a means to a meal. It is a gratifying, even ennobling sort of work, engaging both the mind and the muscles.

— Paraphrased from MICHAEL POLLAN'S
NYT comments on Julia Child

Cooking is primarily fun…the more people know what they are doing, the more fun it is.

—JAMES BEARD

Cooking is fundamental to our humanity.

—MICHAEL RUHLMAN

Eat anything you want—just as long as you're willing to cook it yourself.

—HARRY BALZER

Cooking for people's pleasure is obviously a nice thing to do, but the Number One reason we eat is to nourish ourselves and take care of ourselves.

—SAM KASS

You want to have an infatuation with the ingredients you cook with.

—MICHAEL ANTHONY

A recipe has no soul. You, as the cook, must bring soul to the recipe.

—THOMAS KELLER

I don't like gourmet cooking or 'this' cooking or 'that' cooking. I like good cooking.

—JAMES BEARD

The kitchen is a country in which there are always discoveries to be made.

—GRIMOD DE LA REYNIÈRE

The interaction of ingredients—which differs from day to day—the mood of the cook, the functioning of the equipment, even the weather on the day the recipe is put down onto paper combine to dictate a particular formula. Thus a recipe is only the expression of one moment in time, and that moment can never be exactly duplicated...

—JACQUES PÉPIN

It is our national responsibility to cook and to eat well.

—FRANÇOISE BRANGET

What I love about cooking is that after a hard day, there is something comforting about the fact that if you melt butter and add flour and then hot stock, it will get thick! It's a sure thing! It's a sure thing in a world where nothing is sure; it has a mathematical certainty in a world where those of us who long for some kind of certainty are forced to settle for crossword puzzles.

—NORA EPHRON

The preparation, cooking, and eating of food is a sacrament. Treating it as such has the potential to elevate the quality of our daily lives like nothing else.

—KAREN PAGE &
ANDREW DORNENBURG

To create a dish, one starts with an idea and a number of ingredients...The goal is not to punctiliously follow instructions on a printed page; the goal is to duplicate a taste.

—JACQUES PÉPIN

Whenever we cook we become practical chemists, drawing on the fine accumulated knowledge of generations, and transforming what the Earth offers us into more concentrated forms of pleasure and nourishment.

—FROM A 17TH CENTURY WOODCUT

Imagine keeping it simple: no fuss, flavorful meals, warm conversation, celebration. What could be more satisfying? When you realize that *real* cooking is not about what you cook, but why you cook, then you have discovered healthy food. Sustainably grown, local foods are great choices as these growers are personally invested in their products. Most importantly, though, healthy food is food that you are passionate about cooking and that brings joy to your table. Eat, enjoy, breathe.

—MAGGIE EWING

There are no stupid questions in the kitchen.

—SOPHIE DUDEMAINE

If you can read, you can cook.

—JULIA CHILD

Ultimately, cooking offers the opportunity to be immersed in one's senses and in the moment like no other activity, uniting the inner and outer selves.

—KAREN PAGE &
ANDREW DORNENBURG

I cook to comprehend a place I've landed in.

—ANNIA CIEZADLO

The act of cooking is the bridge between nature and culture.

—MICHAEL POLLAN

I watch cooking change the cook, just as it transforms the food.

—LAURA ESQUIVEL

You don't have to cook fancy or complicated masterpieces; just good food from fresh ingredients.

—JULIA CHILD

# Dining

*Dining is an act of elegance, incorporating the necessity of eating with the graciousness of the host(ess) and the sublime art of the table. It is a celebration, during which the sum of the experience is more than its parts. Here, naturalist Wendell Berry and poet Maya Angelou join culinary icons in expressing their insights into this act which ever sustains us.*

First we eat, then we do everything else.

—M.F.K. FISHER

Eating with the fullest pleasure—pleasure, that is, that does not depend on ignorance—is perhaps the profoundest enactment of our connection with the world.

—WENDELL BERRY

The French treat every meal as something special. Setting one's table can be nearly as important as preparing the food. It focuses the mind on what lies ahead and whets the appetite, opening it to a fuller experience.

—MIREILLE GUILIANO

Food is one of the greatest mediums to touch people. It speaks to us on so many levels: social, emotional and spiritual. I like to show the food the respect that it deserves in the kitchen and that my patrons deserve in the dining room. That's what I think about when I make gumbo.

—FRANK BRIGTSEN

Food is physical, psychological and emotional. There's almost nothing like it as both a connector and a divider.

—WILLIAM J. DOHERTY

In France, one dines. Everywhere else, one eats.

—MONTESQUIEU

We live now in the world of the generic apple, in large part because our taste buds have gone generic. Cultivating ourselves is the first step toward re-diversifying the fields and orchards around us.

—VERLYN KLINKENBORG

The fabric of our lives is bound in the food that we eat and the way we sit down to eat.

—MAIRA KALMAN

One of the very nicest things about life is the way we must regularly stop whatever it is we are doing and devote our attention to eating.

—LUCIANO PAVAROTTI &
WILLIAM WRIGHT

Food is like sex. When done well, it engages all five senses; it taps into our most primal needs and urges and it's among the greatest pleasures you can experience. And like sex, eating good food is a celebration, and an affirmation of life.

—DR. JOHN LA PUMA

The pleasures of the table are considered sensations born of the various circumstances of fact, things, and persons accompanying the meal.

—BRILLAT-SAVARIN

You don't need a silver fork to eat good food.

—PAUL PRUDHOMME

It's difficult to think anything but pleasant thoughts while eating a homegrown tomato.

—LEWIS GRIZZARD

Memory resides in the gut.

—JOE SCULLY

Eating is so intimate. It's very sensual. When you invite someone to sit at your table and you want to cook for them, you're inviting a person into your life.

—MAYA ANGELOU

Eating is sensorial. More than that, it's about interpreting the information that your senses give you.

—CHEF ANDONI

It was the meal which was responsible for the birth, or at least the elaboration of languages, not only because it was a continually recurring occasion for meetings, but also because the leisure which accompanies and succeeds the meal is naturally conducive to confidence and loquacity.

—BRILLAT-SAVARIN

Gourmandism is an impassioned, reasoned, and habitual preference for everything which gratifies the organ of taste.

—BRILLAT-SAVARIN

Food is our common ground, a universal experience.

—JAMES BEARD

People who love to eat are always the best people.

—JULIA CHILD

# Wine

*What would a meal be without wine? (Breakfast, perhaps?) This most elevated elixir, the juice of the vine, has sustained man throughout the ages and given him reason to sing and wax poetic, as well as being the perfect foil for all the ingredients you could ever set on your plate. Here Galileo, Johann Strauss, Benjamin Franklin, and Pope Pius XII among others, reflect on the joys of this unequaled beverage.*

Wine is sunlight held together by water.

—GALILEO

Wine, the most delightful of drinks, whether we owe it to Noah, who planted the vine, or to Bacchus, who pressed juice from the grape, dates from the childhood of the world; and beer, which is attributed to Osiris, goes back to a period beyond which nothing certain is known.

—BRILLAT-SAVARIN

We drink wine not to dull our senses, but to awaken them.

—MIREILLE GUILIANO

Wine is one of the most civilized things in the world and one of the most natural things of the world that has been brought to the greatest perfection, and it offers a greater range for enjoyment and appreciation than, possibly, any other purely sensory thing.

—ERNEST HEMINGWAY

Champagne gives the impression that every day is Sunday.

—MARLENE DIETRICH

Wine is food.

—MARK ROSENSTEIN

Champagne celebrates life. We should be drinking it every day and at every opportunity.

—CAROL DUVAL-LEROY

Wine makes daily living easier, less hurried, with fewer tensions and more tolerance.

—BENJAMIN FRANKLIN

Food without wine is a corpse; wine without food is a ghost. United and well matched, they are as body and soul: living partners.

—ANDRÉ SIMON

By a just compensation, the act of drinking may in certain circumstances provide us with the keenest pleasure; and when a terrible thirst is quenched, or a moderate thirst allayed by some delicious drink, the whole papillary apparatus is titillated, from the tip of the tongue to the depths of the stomach.

—BRILLAT-SAVARIN

Wine: poetry you can taste.

—GERALD ASHER

Burgundy is a way of life.

—STEVE PIGNATIELLO

Cherish good wines for they are the dream makers of the seeds of your goals.

—UNKNOWN

A waltz and a glass of wine invite an encore.

—JOHANN STRAUSS

Wine is a friend, wine is a joy; and, like sunshine, wine is the birthright of all.

—ANDRÉ SIMON

Nothing more excellent or valuable than wine was ever granted by the Gods to man.

—PLATO

Wine in itself is an excellent thing.

—POPE PIUS XII

Food, like the people who eat it, can be stimulated by wine or spirits.

—JULIA CHILD

One barrel of wine can work more miracles than a church full of saints.

—ITALIAN PROVERB

Great food and great produce is incomplete without great wine.

—ANDRE URSINI

A day without wine is like a day without sunshine.

—FRENCH SAYING

Wine to me is passion. It's family and friends. It's warmth of heart and generosity of spirit. Wine is art. It's culture. It's the essence of civilization and the art of living.

—ROBERT MONDAVI

Beer is made by men, wine by God.

—MARTIN LUTHER

Alcohol is a misunderstood vitamin.

—P.G. WODEHOUSE

Sorrow can be alleviated by good sleep, a bath and a glass of good wine.

—SAINT THOMAS AQUINAS

Age and glasses of wine should never be counted.

—UNKNOWN

# *Community*

*The individuals who make up our community—those who have nourished us since our beginnings and who stand up next to us at landmark occasions, as well as those whose faces we see in passing at the supermarket or in the lunch line or at town meetings—these are the fabric of our lives, threads interwoven with our own, making us stronger, more colorful, reminding us that we are all individuals, and yet we are more than that when we stand side-by-side. Food is a great equalizer, a common necessity and a common joy. We can empathize with our neighbor when we understand what is on his plate. Join Carême, Thich Nhat Hanh, Tolkien and others in their reflections on what draws us all together.*

I think of food as a bridge to understanding people.

—MARK MILLER

There has never been a great event, which was not conceived, worked out, and organized over a meal.

—BRILLAT-SAVARIN

One of life's greatest pleasures is enjoying our food and the company of friends and family.

—DR. JOHN LA PUMA

Eating a meal in mindfulness is an important practice. We turn off the TV, put down our newspaper, and work together for five or ten minutes, setting the table and finishing whatever needs to be done. During these few minutes, we can be very happy. When the food is on the table and everyone is seated, we practice breathing...We look at each person as we breathe in and out in order to be in touch with ourselves and everyone at the table. We don't need two hours to see another person. If we are really settled within ourselves, we only need to look for one or two seconds, and that is enough to see.

—THICH NHAT HANH

We do not sit down at table to eat, but to eat together.

—LYCURGUS

Meals have become a means of government, and the fate of nations has often been sealed at a banquet.

—BRILLAT-SAVARIN

When we no longer have good cooking in the world, we will have no literature, nor high and sharp intelligence, nor friendly gatherings, nor social harmony.

—MARIE-ANTOINE CARÊME

*A tavola non si invecchia.* (At the table with good friends and family, you do not become old.)

—ITALIAN SAYING

When...we speak about things that nourish our awareness of the food and our being together, we cultivate the kind of happiness that is necessary for us to grow.

—THICH NHAT HANH

Food to a large extent is what holds a society together, and eating is closely linked to deep spiritual experiences.

—PETER FARB &
GEORGE ARMELAGOS

The dinner table is the center for the teaching and practicing not just of table manners but of conversation, consideration, tolerance, family feeling, and just about all the other accomplishments of polite society except the minuet.

—JUDITH MARTIN

One of the delights of life is eating with friends, second to that is talking about eating. And, for an unsurpassed double whammy, there is talking about eating while you are eating with friends.

—LAURIE COLWIN

Food is symbolic of love when words are inadequate.

—ALAN D. WOLFERT

The table establishes a kind of tie between the two parties to a discussion.

—BRILLAT-SAVARIN

Food is of vital importance to everyone on the planet, regardless of their age, gender, or religious affiliation. Not just because it sustains our bodies, but it fills our souls, and serves as a platform for social communion.

— ERIK WOLF

If more of us valued food and cheer and song above hoarded gold, it would be a merrier world.

—J.R.R. TOLKIEN

Sharing food with another human being is an intimate act that should not be indulged in lightly.

—M.F.K. FISHER

Food, far more than sex, is the great leveler. Just as every king, prophet, warrior, and saint has a mother, so every Napoleon, every Einstein, every Jesus has to eat.

—BETTY FUSSELL

Food is more than just fuel: It's ritual, celebration, and entertainment.

—JOE SCULLY

To me, food is as much about the moment, the occasion, the location and the company as it is about the taste.

—HESTON BLUMENTHAL

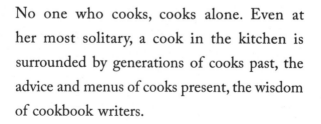

No one who cooks, cooks alone. Even at her most solitary, a cook in the kitchen is surrounded by generations of cooks past, the advice and menus of cooks present, the wisdom of cookbook writers.

—LAURIE COLWIN

If you really want to make a friend, go to someone's house and eat with him…the people who give you their food give you their heart.

—CESAR CHAVEZ

# Art

*There is no art greater than that of creating a work of love—which may be devoured in one instant and never seen again—with the faith that what we have poured into it will remain memorable to those who fleetingly gazed upon it, and then turn it into fuel for a subsequent work of art. Here, Auguste Escoffier, Hervé This, Ruth Reichl and Eric Ripert among others, bring our attention to the art of the plate.*

In the planning of the perfect meal there is art; and after all, is not art the one real, the one important thing in life?

—ELIZABETH ROBINS PENNELL

Good cooking is an art, as well as a form of intense pleasure ... A recipe is only a theme, which an intelligent cook can play each time with a variation.

—MADAME JEHANE BENOÎT

A good meal must be as harmonious as a symphony and as well-constructed as a cathedral.

—FERNAND POINT

With dance music—as with food—you go from simplicity to complexity: strong rhythm, one melody, then another. Dishes can be like that. First fish, then spice, then sauce. In harmony.

—LAURENT MANRIQUE

Gastronomy is the only art which touches our organism in two realms so closely linked—in its psycho-physiological functioning.

—EDOUARD DE POMAINE

The art of cooking…will evolve as a society evolves…only basic rules remain unchangeable.

—AUGUSTE ESCOFFIER

A work of art, particularly a culinary work of art, is also a simplification. The cook makes a choice, and retains those things that best express his idea.

—HERVÉ THIS

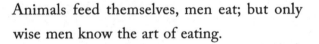

Animals feed themselves, men eat; but only wise men know the art of eating.

—BRILLAT-SAVARIN

Like any fine art, cookery requires taste and creativity, an appreciation of beauty and a mastery of technique.

—SARAH LALANSKY & ALAN HAUSE

When I go to a concert, I think of the notes as flavors.

—RUTH REICHL

A chef's role is almost like a conductor of an orchestra. He does not play one instrument. Rather, he makes sure the whole ensemble works correctly together, each instrument doing its part, to create the "music" that wafts into the front of the house.

—ERIC RIPERT

Magical dishes, magical words: A great cook is, when all is said and done, a great poet.

—MARCEL GRANCHER

With the seven notes of the musical scale one can compose millions of different musical symphonies. With the far more numerous notes of the culinary scale one ought to be able to compose millions of culinary symphonies.

—EDOUARD DE POMAINE

Cookery is not chemistry. It is an art. It requires instinct and taste rather than exact measurements.

—MARCEL BOULESTIN

Ingredients are not sacred. The art of cuisine is sacred.

—TANITH TYRR

Food to the cook is just like marble to Michelangelo: it is up to the artist to bring out what is already there.

—UNKNOWN

*La cuisine est l'art de transformer instantanément en joie des produits chargées d'histoire.* (Cooking is the art of instantly transforming history-laden products into joy.)

—GUY SAVOY

Cookery is a wholly unselfish art: All good cooks, like all great artists, must have an audience worth cooking for.

—ANDRÉ SIMON

The rhythm of our food derives from the surrounding landscape, the cultures and the traditions that give food its beauty, tastes and aromas…Rhythm requires an appreciation of pleasure, of the harmony of food, its inner meaning. A great food experience is the result of an art that conceals art, a wonderful synchronicity of the material and non-material worlds.

—IACP

Cooking is become an art, a noble science.

—ROBERT BURTON

An artist is never poor.

—BABETTE'S FEAST

# Spirit

*The pursuit of cooking, dining, sharing and cele-
brating is so much more than the nuts and bolts
of feeding our body. It is the spirit with which we
gather our food, sit down to eat, offer up thanks,
embrace those around us, and vow to "give it forth"
as we rise from the table. Join the reflections of
Edouard de Pomaine, Harriet Van Horne, Molly
O'Neill, Judith Jones, and others as they sing of
that which weaves all elements together.*

The discovery of a new dish does more for the happiness of mankind than the discovery of a star.

—BRILLAT-SAVARIN

Cooking demands attention, patience, and above all, respect for the gifts of the earth. It is a form of worship, a way of giving thanks.

—JUDITH B. JONES

Bouillon is the soul of the household.

—JULES GOUFFÉ

Cooking like an Indian means cooking as you live, working out a balance, filling it with spice, and always looking at what your hands produce as something beyond the individual ingredients, as a story and a gift, and as something that perhaps should always remain a bit of a mystery.

—MICHAEL ROBERTS

This is my advice to people: Learn how to cook, try new recipes, learn from your mistakes, be fearless, and above all have fun!

—JULIA CHILD

Music touches the spirit, whilst cooking touches not merely the spirit but the whole of our physiological economy as well.

—EDOUARD DE POMAINE

Cooking is like love; it should be entered into with abandon or not at all.

—HARRIET VAN HORNE

At the end of a good dinner, body and soul both enjoy a remarkable sense of well-being.

—BRILLAT-SAVARIN

Life is so brief that we should not glance either too far backwards or forwards ... therefore study how to fix our happiness in our glass and in our plate.

—GRIMOD DE LA REYNIÈRE

Find something you're passionate about and keep tremendously interested in it.

—JULIA CHILD

The senses are the portals to the mind.

—MIREILLE GUILIANO

People who choose a career in the culinary arts are almost always driven by their passion: the desire to create something extraordinary that gives others pleasure; the instinct to serve people with pride; and the simple joy of making people happy from the inside out. These are not things one decides to do on a whim. For most of us, this is a calling of the highest order, and one that can only be answered by spending every day doing what we love.

—DOROTHY HAMILTON

A love of food, cooking and mealtimes comes from within.

—LOUISE LUIGGI

A good cook is like a sorceress who dispenses happiness.

—ELSA SCHIAPARELLI

To define the moment of a cuisine's birth is an attempt to describe the spirit of a people, the ineffable appetite that is held in common, undiminished by time.

—MOLLY O'NEILL

Recipes don't work unless you use your heart!

—DYLAN JONES

Most seafoods...should be simply threatened with heat and then celebrated with joy.

—JEFF SMITH

Good cheer is far from being harmful to health, and, all things being equal, gourmands live longer than other men.

—BRILLAT-SAVARIN

A good dinner will make anyone smile.

—KRISTINE SOLOMON

In what art or science [other than cooking] could improvements be made that would more powerfully contribute to increase the comforts and enjoyments of mankind?

—SIR BENJAMIN THOMPSON,
COUNT RUMFORD

# Knowledge

'The more you know, the more you know you don't know,' as Jean-Pierre Philippe so eloquently expressed. But the more we know, the more likely we are to end up with a delectable offering for our guests. Join Harold McGee, Nathalie Dupree, Alain Ducasse and Pierre Gagnaire among others, for these reflections on mastery.

Curiosity and understanding make their own contribution to mastery.

—HAROLD MCGEE

Some knowledge of gastronomy is necessary to all men, since it adds to the sum of human pleasures.

—BRILLAT-SAVARIN

There is nothing noble in failing to discover and cultivate your pleasures. You owe it to your loved ones as well as yourself to know and pursue your pleasures.

—MIREILLE GUILIANO

First, knife skills. Then, knowing how to control heat. Most important is choosing the right product...the rest is simple.

—JUSTIN QUEK

The definition of gumbo resides at the intersection of memory, expectation, and experience.

—ELIZABETH PEARCE

In the act of tasting, when the bite or sip moves through the mouth and into the body, culture and nature become one.

—AMY B. TRUBEK

*Je sais, je sais que je [ne] sais jamais.* (I know, I know that I never know.)

   —JEAN-PIERRE PHILIPPE

No one is born a great cook; one learns by doing.

   —JULIA CHILD

We need to learn to look behind what we perceive, to taste behind what we taste.

   —PIERRE GAGNAIRE

The qualities that we aim to influence in the kitchen—taste, aroma, texture, color, nutritiousness—are all manifestations of chemical properties.

—HAROLD MCGEE

Flavor is a language that anyone who loves the pleasures of the palate will find to be well worth mastering. Once you master the language of flavor, you can use it to communicate—and become a better cook.

—KAREN PAGE & ANDREW DORNENBURG

Only when the last tree has been cut down...
Only when the last river has been poisoned...
Only when the last fish has been caught...
Only then will you find that money cannot
be eaten.

—CREE INDIAN PROPHECY

The cook must find a way to produce dishes
that speak to the soul and the mind—not just
in contemplative terms, as it were, as something one likes or dislikes, but in intellectual
terms as well.

—HERVÉ THIS

The great virtue of thought and analysis is that they free us from the necessity of following recipes.

—HAROLD MCGEE

When the French take a bite of cheese or a sip of wine, they taste the earth: rock, grass, hillside, valley, plateau. They combine gustatory sensation and the evocative possibilities of taste in their fidelity to the taste of place, or *goût du terroir*.

—AMY B. TRUBEK

*La cuisine, c'est 60% le produit et 40% la technique!*
(Cooking is 60% product and 40% technique!)

—ALAIN DUCASSE

The destiny of nations depends on the manner
in which they feed themselves.

—BRILLAT-SAVARIN

While a lone chop in a pan is bound to dry
out, two chops will supply each other with the
juice they both need.

—NATHALIE DUPREE

Cooks have always been the world's experts in the applied science of deliciousness.

—HAROLD MCGEE

Secrets, especially with cooking, are best shared so that the cuisine lives on.

—BO SONGVISAVA

Cooking is an observation-based process that you can't do if you're completely focused on a recipe.

—ALTON BROWN

Recipes are family stories, tales of particular places and personal histories. They bear witness to the land and waterways, to technology and invention, to immigration, migration, ambition, disappointment, triumph, and most of all, change.

—MOLLY O'NEILL

Reading and eating should both be done slowly.

—SPANISH PROVERB

To eat is a necessity but to eat intelligently is an art.

—FRANÇOIS DE LA ROCHEFOUCAULD

# Humor

*Who are we without laughter? Whether it's laughter at our own shortcomings and delightful mistakes, or for the well-being which a good burst of rollicking mirth can afford, laughter sustains us perhaps as much as does the food we eat. Join Charles de Gaulle, Oscar Wilde, Ronald Reagan, Dolly Parton and others in their outrageous reflections upon the humor of food.*

I come from a family where gravy is considered a beverage.

—ERMA BOMBECK

The only two things I don't eat for breakfast are lunch and dinner.

—UNKNOWN

The primary requisite for writing well about food is a good appetite.

—A. J. LIEBLING

Fish, to taste right, must swim three times: in water, in butter and in wine.

—POLISH PROVERB

Tomatoes and oregano make it Italian; wine and tarragon make it French; soy sauce makes it Chinese; garlic makes it good.

—ALICE MAY BROCK

If it has four legs and it's not a table, eat it.

—CANTONESE SAYING

Without ice cream, there would be darkness and chaos.

—DON KARDONG

How can I govern a country which has 246 varieties of cheese?

—CHARLES DE GAULLE

You can tell a lot about a fellow's character by his way of eating jellybeans.

—RONALD REAGAN

There's nothing better than a good friend, except a good friend with chocolate.

—LINDA GRAYSON

I think every woman should have a blowtorch.

—JULIA CHILD

A man is in general better pleased when he has a good dinner upon the table than when his wife talks Greek.

—SAMUEL JOHNSON

A balanced diet is a cookie in each hand.

—BARBARA JOHNSON

After a good dinner one can forgive anybody, even one's own relatives.

—OSCAR WILDE

Twenty minutes in the kitchen will save you three hours on the StairMaster.

—DEVIN ALEXANDER

You first parents of the human race ... who ruined yourself for an apple, what might you have done for a truffled turkey?

—BRILLAT-SAVARIN

Everything you see, I owe to spaghetti.

—SOPHIA LOREN

Life is a combination of magic and pasta.

—FEDERICO FELLINI

Food is life. The rest is parsley.

—ALAN RICHMAN

I look upon it that he who does not mind his belly will hardly mind anything else.

—SAMUEL JOHNSON

Our lives are not in the lap of the Gods, but in the lap of our cooks.

—LIN YUTANG

A party without cake is just a meeting.

—JULIA CHILD

My weaknesses have always been food and men—in that order.

—DOLLY PARTON

A home cook who relies too much on a recipe is sort of like a pilot who reads the plane's instruction manual while flying.

—ALTON BROWN

Smell and taste are in fact but a single sense, whose laboratory is the mouth and whose chimney is the nose.

—BRILLAT-SAVARIN

The only time to eat diet food is while you are waiting for the steak to cook.

—JULIA CHILD

Life is uncertain. Eat dessert first.

—ERNESTINE ULMER

# *Essence*

*When we distill things down to the bare essentials—when we cut out any extraneous baggage and consider why we are here and what makes us happy—we are left with thoughts such as these. Join Colette, Curnonsky, Miguel de Cervantes and Anthony Bourdain among others, as they reflect upon that which ultimately makes us tick.*

Pull up a chair. Take a taste. Come join us. Life is so endlessly delicious.

—RUTH REICHL

Things are good when they taste like what they are.

—CURNONSKY

Civilization defines itself by the rituals of everyday life.

—MIREILLE GUILIANO

When we eat, we experience an indefinable and peculiar sensation of well-being, arising out of an instinctive awareness that through what we are eating we are repairing our losses and prolonging our existence.

—BRILLAT-SAVARIN

*Le vrai gourmet est celui qui se délecte d'une tartine de beurre comme d'un homard grillé, si le beurre est fin et le pain bien pétri.*

(The real gourmet is one who enjoys a slice of bread and butter as much as a grilled lobster, if the butter is fine and the bread well-kneaded.)

—COLETTE

Ayurvedic principles call for six tastes—salty, sweet, bitter, sour, astringent, and pungent—to be included, and for harmony among the elements to achieve good health. If the body's system is out of balance, an emphasis on a certain taste might bring things back into alignment.

—MICHAEL ROBERTS

The pleasures of the table belong to all times and all ages, to every country and every day; they go hand in hand with all our other pleasures, outlast them, and remain to console us for their loss.

—BRILLAT-SAVARIN

A morsel of fine cheese is a rich meditation on maturity, the fulfillment of possibility, the way of all flesh.

—HAROLD MCGEE

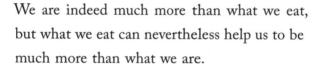

We are indeed much more than what we eat, but what we eat can nevertheless help us to be much more than what we are.

—CRAIG MARTIN

The stomach is where your true feelings are.

—AMY TAN

Thoughtful cooking means paying attention to what our senses tell us as we prepare it.

—HAROLD MCGEE

There are three items that can provide nourishment and energy for positive change: the air you breathe, the food you eat, and the ideas you ponder.

—MARK MILLER

The greatest dishes are very simple.

—AUGUSTE ESCOFFIER

The cooking that I dream of…must give happiness, emotion.

—PIERRE GAGNAIRE

The pleasure of eating is the actual and direct sensation of a need being satisfied.

—BRILLAT-SAVARIN

Cooking has two purposes: nourishing the body and nourishing the mind.

—HERVÉ THIS

The manner in which meals are conducted is an important ingredient in the happiness of life.

—BRILLAT-SAVARIN

Flavors are something like chemical chords, composite sensations built up from notes provided by different molecules.

—HAROLD MCGEE

I try to make dishes evoke worlds, colors, feelings.

—PIERRE GAGNAIRE

One of the pleasantest of all emotions is to know that I, I with my brain and my hands, have nourished my beloved few, that I have concocted a stew or a story, a rarity or a plain dish, to sustain them truly against the hungers of the world.

—M.F.K. FISHER

So long as you have food in your mouth you have solved all questions for the time being.

—FRANZ KAFKA

All sorrows are less with bread.

—MIGUEL DE CERVANTES

Anyone who's a chef, who loves food, ultimately knows that all that matters is: "Is it good? Does it give pleasure?"

—ANTHONY BOURDAIN

Cooking…is an activity that strikes a deep emotional chord in us, one that might even go to the heart of our identity as human beings.

—MICHAEL POLLAN

Tell me what you eat; I will tell you what you are.

—BRILLAT-SAVARIN

# *Love*

*There is no greater verse than 1 Corinthians 13:13: "And now these three remain: faith, hope and love. But the greatest of these is love." French molecular gastronomist Hervé This has dedicated his life to the scientific researching of what makes a meal great, and has come to the ultimate conclusion that cooking is love. Join This, along with Alain Chapel, Virginia Woolf, George Bernard Shaw and others, as they reiterate this essential message.*

Flour, salt, pepper, love; those are the ingredients you need for gravy.

—MARTHA HAWKINS

Making and enjoying good food is not a matter of class or wealth or education or race. It is a matter of heart.

—LIZ WILLIAMS

In the hands of a great cook, a meal is capable of touching us as a love song does, of giving us joy, occasionally even moving us to anger.

—HERVÉ THIS

*La véritable mission de la cuisine consiste à donner de l'amour.*
(The true mission of cuisine consists in transmitting love.)

—HERVÉ THIS

In the unconscious mind, food equals love because food is our deepest and earliest connection with our caretaker.

—KATHRYN ZERBE

Of soups and love, the first is best.

—SPANISH PROVERB

It is not food we're hungry for; we're hungry for the love of the person who's cooking.

—HERVÉ THIS

I am hungry...our three basic needs, for food and security and love, are so mixed and mingled and entwined that we cannot straightly think of one without the others.

—M.F.K. FISHER

One cannot think well, love well, sleep well if one has not dined well.

—VIRGINIA WOOLF

No matter how you slice and dice it, food and love are inextricably tied.

—KRISTINE SOLOMON

There is a feeling of love in the giving of comfort.

—JOE SCULLY

You have to love either what you are going to eat, or the person you are cooking for. Then you have to give yourself up to cooking. Cuisine is an act of love.

—ALAIN CHAPEL

Cooking is love made visible.

—BARRY POPIK

There is no love sincerer than the love of food.

—GEORGE BERNARD SHAW

Food can be very transformational, and it can be more than just about a dish. That's what happened to me when I first went to France. I fell in love. And if you fall in love, well, then everything is easy.

—ALICE WATERS

Cooking is one of the great gifts you can give to those you love.

—INA GARTEN

The main thing…is the love of the person who cooks for you, and the love of those who share the meal with you.

—HERVÉ THIS

Food tastes better when you eat it with someone you love.

—UNKNOWN

Cookies are made of butter and love.

—NORWEGIAN PROVERB

Our palates are our passports.

—JIM WAGNER

There is no sight on earth more appealing than the sight of a woman making dinner for someone she loves.

—THOMAS WOLFE

Isn't cooking first and foremost a matter of love?

—HERVÉ THIS

# *In Closing: A Lagniappe*

I N L O U I S I A N A ,  T H E  S P I R I T  of a little something extra is summed up in the word *"lagniappe"*, a French Creole expression for gift. While we may not always have the ingredients on hand to confect a fine meal, be it due to hard times or a distance from resources, we always have the capacity to enjoy whatever is set before us.

My hope in the sharing of this selection of culinary quotes is that you will take what you have and savor it to its fullest. Share it

if possible, and never forget the wisdom of
Brillat-Savarin:

"You are what you eat!"

—Susi Gott Séguret
*Shelton Laurel, NC*